(D.... you.

Love

SUN SKY SEA
and Sometimes
MUD!

Enjoy

Sus Lavern

Dec 17/23

BY JOAN LAVERN
MARSHALL WILKINSON

ILLUSTRATIONS BY KANO MAC

◆ FriesenPress

One Printers Way
Altona, MB R0G 0B0
Canada

www.friesenpress.com

Contributors: Verlyne V. Forde, Cheril Marshall-Morris
& Colvin Jabez Marshall

Illustrations by Kano Mac

Nursery Rhymes used are for the sole and only purpose of depicting how we spent moonlight nights playing children's games, having fun. and entertaining ourselves. Some of the nursery rhymes were learned at school or generational; that is, we would have heard them from someone older than we were, or they would have been sung or taught to us by older family members.

ISBN
978-1-03-915328-8 (Hardcover)
978-1-03-915327-1 (Paperback)
978-1-03-915329-5 (eBook)

1. POETRY, CARIBBEAN & LATIN AMERICAN

Distributed to the trade by The Ingram Book Company

Map of Barbados

Dedicated to The Sobers Tree

PAST
    PRESENT
        FUTURE

INTRODUCTION

I hope you will enjoy this volume of poems—*Sun, Sky, Sea, and Sometimes Mud.*

The book's title is an acknowledgement of the God-given gifts we enjoyed as children. We did not see them as gifts at the time. They were just there, and we took them for granted.

Some would have us believe that all we had was poverty. It was the excess that we may have seen from outsiders that made us feel poor, but most of us had what was required to exist.

If we went to sleep hungry, it was because we were too lazy to go make some crispy bakes or a glass of refreshing lemonade, or brew a cup of hot Fry's Cocoa, or butter some crispy Eclipse or Soda biscuits.

We were the begotten of the generation of parents who started immigrating in the early 1950s and '60s to find greener pastures in the mother country (England). They could not be sure of what awaited them, so they flew solo and left, us, their children, in the care of their parents, our grandparents.

This afforded us the best of both worlds.

Grandparents who were now wiser than when they raised their own children: more tolerant and easy-going—not prone to share as many lashes (licks); more focused and more determined to catapult us to a higher and more thorough education.

The money our immigrant parents would earn and send back to Barbados would certainly give us an advantage and the opportunity to attend high school. Education in Barbados was free, but there were uniforms, shoes, books to be purchased, bus fare to be paid, lunch, school fees, and other incidentals that added up.

An astronomical amount especially when there were seven children to feed, clothe, shelter and educate. It would have been impossible to do all this on a conventional Barbadian salary.

Our only uncle was the first to take leave of Barbados, and one of my aunts soon followed.

In the fullness of time, my dad was encouraged to also give the immigrant life a try and he left for England. He sent for our mom soon after. We were left in the care of our grandparents and an aunt who was young enough to be an older sister, but we did not realize that until much, much later. Our maternal grandparents, along with our Aunt Jan (Janet), were the main caregivers and guardians, but our paternal grandparents were also a part of our lives.

And so, began our formative life in the land of

Sun, Sky, Sea and Sometimes Mud.

Dedicated to all of us who were ever called Mud.

Gifts from the most high.

Gifts that will outlast money, clothing, riches, the material things that are fleeting. Intrinsic values.

The intention is for each poem to be pastoral, to bring a sense of awareness, a sense of belonging and take your mind's eye back to childhood:

The joys

The tears

The laughter

Life could have been complex, but we lived simple lives. Humble and respectful to nature and all it offered.

Sun:	brightness, warmth, joy, love
Sky:	aspirations, freedom, infinity
Sea:	fear, uncertainty, change, doubt, possibility, reverence
Mud:	creation, foundation, growth, bliss, innocence

The beauty of nature.

The innocence and serenity of it all.

Is there anything more glorious than:

Waking up to the sun rise or watching the sun set?

Looking up to the heavens and seeing the blue sky and those white puffy clouds dancing, frolicking, skylarking.

Beholding the *sea*—that vast expanse of water, wondering where it starts and ends. Does it ever get weary?

Mud, that black, rich substance. Without it, nothing will grow. Isn't everything held together by mud? Isn't it the glue of the earth? Wasn't the first man made from mud; the genesis of man?

What untold pleasure we had as kids, playing in mud. Squeezing that gooey substance between our toes and jumping up and down with pleasure. Making our footprint in the mud, knowing that it would stay until a rain came. Not fleeting like the ones we made in the sand, which would be washed away with the flow and ebb of the tide.

The grown-up feeling, experiences when we made mud cakes or mud pies and left them in the sun to bake. No cost involved.

All God-given resources freely bestowed on us—mud, water, and a piece of stick.

Stir and mix and leave to bake (in the sun).

Few hours later, you behold the fruit of your labour. A perfectly made mud cake. Few hours later, add water again, and that cake is back to its original form—the beauty of mud.

Is there anything else, any other matter, so flexible, so pliable?

We used mud to make our cricket stumps. We would pack the mud together, nice and solid. Three nice piles, and we were ready to play cricket or bat and ball, one of our favourite childhood games.

For we, who are dark-skinned, we are often referred to as Mud.

We feel insulted and, as children, it hurt to the core, to be called Mud.

We were too naïve to realize the importance of MUD.

Out of the mud we came, and back to the mud, we will go.

Mud is dug and heaped to the side of our grave—our final resting place.

We are lowered into the grave and covered by MUD.

Sun, Sea, Sky, and Sometimes Mud.

Table of Contents

Bequests

Sun
Sky
Sea

Mud

Intrinsic gifts
Of Love

Bestowed
On us

From

God

Above

—JLM

Life's Wonderful

The sea

Ain't got no backdoor
One of our ole folklore

So we stay out of the water
And play on the shore

Watch the tides come and go

Embracing
Plying
Enjoying

The sand
In
With
Our hands

Building sandcastles
       Razzle
              Dazzle

Puffy white clouds
Frolicking

The sky

Cuddling them

The sun

Enjoying it all

Smiling loud

Life's wonderful.

—JLM

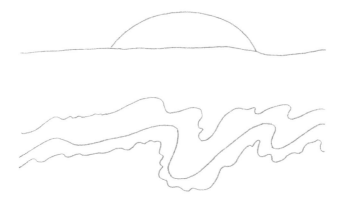

Mom & Dad

Our parents must have shed many tears
Being absent during our formative years

But that was their sacrifice
To give us a better life

They lived up to their responsibility
Supported us monetarily and financially

A birthday was never forgotten
A gift always arrived from England

A watch
A bracelet
A ring

A five or ten-pound note
Enclosed in the letters they wrote

They sent parcels with goodies
English mints, candies, toffees

Parcels arrived with things that were unique
Different, fascinating, and also antique

Transistor radio shaped like a violin
Complete with bow and strings

A novelty all in one ballpoint pen
Ink colours of black, blue, red, green

How special were all these things
We felt like queens and kings

Embraced the life we knew

Were we mad
Were we sad

Did we feel a sense of regret
Parental abandonment or neglect

We acknowledge their sacrifice
To give us a better life?

We romped and played in the sun
Had a glorious childhood of fun

Experienced the love of extended family
From grandparents uncle and aunties

Grew up with a moral and sound foundation
Received a solid high school education

We enjoyed the best of both worlds
If the truth be told

Are we mad
Are we sad

Do we feel a sense of regret
Parental abandonment or neglect?

We acknowledge their sacrifice
To give us a better life

Circumstances may have kept us apart
They had our best interest at heart.

Colvin McDonald (Dad)
Catherine McLean (Mom)

—JLM

Sunday Morning

Yes!
There was something

About Sunday mornings

The aroma of
My grandmother's cooking

Early in the morning
A new day dawning

ECAF coffee brewing

Oh, so intoxicating

Tickling our nostril

While we stayed still

The quiet in the house

We'd settle back in bed

Snuggle back to sleep

Wrapped

In a blanket

Of

Comfort
Reassurance
Safety
Love

—JLM

My Grandfathers

Tall and willowy
Agile
Lively

Local comedians
Telling Barbadians

Stories

With humour
And glee

Worked
Every day

Sometimes
Without pay

Toiled
The Soil

Provided
For
Their families

Were
Leaders in the
Communities

Showed they cared

Always shared

Knew no fear
Undertakings sincere

Full
Of
Energy and vigour

Men of character

Everybody
Liked them

They
Were decent
Men   loving grandfathers

I Loved Her So

She seemed to fret all day
Wanting everything her way

Now

I realized she was not mean
It was her desire to have things neat 'n clean

Rejecting disorder and disarray
Demanding that dishes be washed and packed away

Not a speck of dust on the floor
Everyone expected to complete their given chore

School uniforms washed and pressed
We were always fashionable and well dressed

She combed and fixed our hair with pride
Ribbons and bows always perfectly tied

Clothing purchased for the boys was versatile
They were always fashionable and in style

Meals were always worth the wait
Beautifully arranged on every plate

Dumplings was one of her specialities
Loved and enjoyed by the whole family

As her parents
Our grandparents
Got older
Their care fell on her shoulder

She was kind and caring
Truly one of God's blessings

We received one-of-a-kind care
                    I
Will forever keep her memory dear

Words cannot convey what she meant to me
I will cherish her for eternity   my Aunt Jan

Aunts 'N Uncle

Parents cannot do it all
Especially when you are small

So God blessed us with extended family
Who also provided support and helped financially

Sending parcels and money from overseas
That purchased provisions for lots of our meals

Christmas time those postcards would arrive
British pounds and Canadian dollars tucked inside

Those aunts who lived on the island
Were attentive engaged and reliant.

We look back with gratitude in our hearts
Loving them for doing their part

We always knew we were blessed
Our aunts and uncle were the best

De Crocus Bag

Don't ever say de crocus bag
Is just a piece uh rag

Our enslaved ancestors fashioned them into garments
Back then Massa said it was their allotment

We used it to mop the wooden floor
It was a welcome mat at every door

If there was a heavy load to carry
There was no need to fret or worry

Bunch of coconuts attached by the stem
Could be wrapped controllably in one of them

Make a pad and put that bundle on your head
Or sling it over the shoulder instead

De crocus bag was shipped with provisions
Every one of us with childish ambition

Taking the patience and time
To unthread the interwinding twine

Working at it was like an obsession
Intending to make it a prized possession

When it was time for our fun and games
There was always that Race of Fame

Who could jump de fastest in a crocus sack
On the local grass or a dirt track

That crocus bag was a part of our past

Durable
Flexible
Useful

Made to last

—JLM

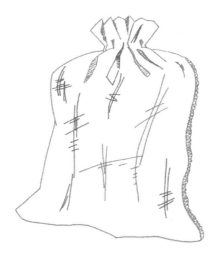

The Glass Cup

Coconut water 'n Fruitee
Beverage on Sundays.
Served in De Special Glass Cup
Always locked up in De Cabinet

If company came by
For sure it came outside.
Other than that it was on display
Touch it we did not dare

Look how it sparkles 'n shine
They have had it for a long time
Wonder how much it must have cost
Breaking it, would be a great loss

Imagine the sacrifices made
Blood and tears our parents paid
To attain the finer things in life
Amid life's struggle and strife

O, how they may have pray and pray
Lord let them give we de lil back pay
Long hours toiling in de hot sun
Was surely not games and fun

And so we glance back with love in our hearts
Understanding and forgiveness we must impart
It was more than a glass cup
On display in de cabinet

Blood sweat and tears
Blood sweat and tears

Swimming against fears

Of generational poverty
Providing for a family

It was more than a glass cup
On display in de cabinet.

A measure of success
Financial progress

Striving to leave a success story
As part of their personal history

Wanting us to be proud of them

—JLM

Mauby

Made from the bark of the colubrina elliptica tree
Natural resource and can be had free

Boiled with cinnamon nutmeg and cloves
Leave to ferment and cool on the stove

There is the main ingredient
Of this local refreshing drink

Bitter, bitter to the taste
So many health benefits encased

A spoonful a day

Keeps

Arthritis
Cholesterol
Constipation
Diabetes
Hypertension

At bay

Amazingly

It's
Also a
Refreshing drink

Add sugar

Optional
Is a dash of
Liquor

Sweetened to taste

Add ice

Let chill

Grab that glass of Mauby

Sip
Drink

A taste of

Paradise

—JLM

Whap, Whap, Whap

De cou-cou stick
Slipper
Switch

Back uh de hand
Belt
Frypan

Hard ears you won't hear
Own way you gine feel

Whap
Whap
Whap

Don't spare de rod
En spoil de chile
School lay by ever since three
Obedience is the key

You need to listen to me
Or you gine end up in Glendairy.

Whap

Bend   de   tree

Whap

When   it   young

Whap, whap, whap

Now stop that crying in hey
Before I give   you   something   to   cry   FOR

Whap
Whap

Whap

Next time
Yuh   won't   get   off
So   easy

Whap
Guh   Long

Whap

—JLM

De Morning Train

I don't remember who started the song
But we sang it loud

They sang it long
Too long

"I'm going up in the morning train
I'm going up in the morning train
I'm going up in the morning train
For the evening train will be too late"

The hand clapping was all in unison
Cymbals

"Step right in and take a seat
Step right in and take a seat
Step right in and take a seat
For the evening train will be too late"

Double knocks on the cymbals
Crescendo
Urgency

It was visible
The train

Was right there

You just had to climb on

My paternal grandmother jumped to her feet
The sound, the music must be so sweet

Started dancing

     Dancing

       Dancing

         Dancing.

           Dancing

             Dancing

Transfixed

Anchored

I bowed my head
Kept it down

Prancing!   Prancing!!   Prancing!!!

I ceased to sing

God

Let her sit down

Dismay
Emboldened my peripheral

Her fingertips
Twirled
The hem of her dress

I could not
Would not
Look up

Dear God
Let her get on the train
And
SIT
TO HELL
DOWN!

God

Was enjoying
The

Dance!

I remember

Everything

Like it was
Yesterday

I am ashamed

That
I

was

ASHAMED

of
my

Grandmother

Dancing

           Her

                    Way

                            To

                                        Freedom

On
The
Morning train.

Sorry
Ma

—JLM

My Neighbourhood

My neighbourhood

Had everything

Kings
Who owned
The shops
The car
The money
Property

They were married to queens
Who were never seen
Not sure if they had thrones
But they worked like drones
Kept a low profile
Hardly came outside

Never saw them

Wear anything fancy
Or attend a party

Go for a drive in the CAR
Or go anywhere FAR

They lived in their kings' shadow
As though their own existence
Did not MATTER

Butchers who slaughtered pigs on Saturdays or Sundays

Early in the fore day morning

Carpenters
Cobblers
Gossipers
Grave diggers
Labourers
Needle workers
Nurses
Nut sellers
Pastors
Politicians
Preachers
Teachers

Cats who lived inside
Dogs who lived outside
Pigs in their pens
Poultry in their runs

Churches
Hospitals
Lodges
Plantations
Rum shops
Schools
Shops
Stores

TREES

Ackee
Apple
Banana

Breadfruit
Coconut
Dunks
Fat pork
Gooseberry
Green pea
Guavas
Mammie apple
Mango
Pear
Plum
Sugar apple
Soursop
Tamarind

Ground provisions

Cassava
Eddoes
Potato
Yam

Kristophene
Okra
Spinach

Some of us lived in

One-room dwellings
Shacks
Chattels
Houses made of wall
With running water

And electricity
Without

Every house had a lamp
Matches
And kerosene oil

A crocus bag
To wipe the floor

A mat at the door

Everyone, everybody

Tried to live in harmony

In my neighbourhood

—JLM

Dogs

Some were tied, chained
Be it sunshine or rain
A small wooden home
At times concealing a bone
Thrown to them days ago
That we could not gnaw anymore
Boiled in soup or sauteed in a stew
They found something on it to chew
Ate the same foods we did
From an old bowl or a saucepan lid

Fancy kennels were home to a few
Complete with a door to walk through
Owners took them walking in the evenings
Keeping them fit and exercising
Canine of the fancier breed
Treated royally and special, indeed
From head to tail their sheen
Spoke of nice food and the required protein
Ate from nice enamel or aluminium bowls
Had shelter from the rain and the cold

Others roam freely to and fro
Sniffing at anyone and everyone's door
Sometimes targeting penned livestock
Only to be pelted with stones or rocks
But there was no time to waste
After the ducks and poultry they chased
The hen sitting protectively over her eggs
Always the target for the coveted spread

In defiance she would rise from her nest
Chasing them with clucks, pecks, and hiss

They were forever on the prowl
Hoping their snarl and howl
Would force people to step back
When they pounced and make to attack
Some were successful in achieving this
And basically lived in canine bliss
Their reputation was well known
No one bother them and left them alone
Passersby were known to get bitten

Especially if they acted frighten

Others would chase after passing cars
Paws hardly touching the asphalt tar
Race with them for a while and turn around
Wagging their tails as they walk back home
Totally exhausted from the adventurous run
They'd close their eyes and lie in the sun

Panting and totally out of breath

As though they were close to death
Yet alert and ready to respond
To any intruder coming around

There was our local homegrown kind
Languorously waiting and easy to find
Walking with their heads hanging low
As though always expectant of a blow
Eyes darting from pillar to post
Suspicious distrustful to the utmost

We call them the Pot Starvers
They hardly if ever found favour

With neighbours or passersby

Who labelled them mangy and sly

And, oh, those concerning times
The female species got out of line
Turned up in the middle of the street
Without warning and in heat
All the males from far and wide appear
Fighting, vying to be, oh, so near
Checking and sniffing her rump
On top of her they would jump

The adults would ask us not to look

And send us to read a book

But man is master of all he beholds
And some sad stories must now be told
For the adults this was a carnal act
Damn animals behaving in public like that

Dogs should know their place

Not messing up the place

Out came the sticks, rocks and water

In an effort to restore law and order

Utter frenzy as they try to run, helter-skelter
Desperately seeking refuge and shelter

There was no need for this cruelty

Dogs don't know anything about modesty

For the adults it was about morals

No arguments, no squabbles

Keep those mating dogs out of sight

It was about what was right

—JLM

De Paling

Shining bright, tall, erect
A sentry on guard

Rusted, bent
Sometimes lots of dents

The Great Divider of Properties
Yet everybody was neighbourly

Always greeting each other

Sharing existing hardships
Developing lasting friendships

Yes, there were loose lips
That would chatter and gossip

Arguments would erupt

A hen would fly the coop

Over de paling

Landing

Leaving prints

On the white shirts bleaching

On de grass

A pig would escape
Barging

Through the gate
Ransacking

Everything on site
Using only his God-given snout

Everyone angrily chasing this pig
Which is having fun and doing a jig

Meanwhile someone grabs a stick
Giving it some unexpected licks

Finally getting it back in its pen
Precious time foolishly spent

De paling

Standing

Tall

Or bent

Witnessing

If it should start telling stories
Many would have more than worries

Cause when the day is all done
And the sun goes down

Lovers will make out on the sly
Hoping there were safe from prying eyes

Leaning on the paling

Invisible eye saw each passionate kiss
Clearly through the darkness that exist

Muted ear listen to every sigh of pleasure
Holding it a secret treasure

Shinning bright

Tall, erect, rusted, bent

De paling

—JLM

Playing by the Moonlight

So what if there were no street lights
We had the moon's light!
Shining from the sky bright as day
When the sun went its way!

A million and one games we can play
Our grandmother watching from her rocking chair

Puss, Puss, Catch a Corner
Just like Little Jack Horner
What about skylarking and telling jokes
Races, rounders or jumping rope

So many fall downs
To choose from

London Bridge
Jack and Jill
Humpty Dumpty
Atishoo, atishoo
They all fall down

We held each other's hand
Spreading out like a fan

There's a brown girl in the ring
Tra la la la la
There's a brown girl in the ring
Tra la la la la la

See muh lil brown girl call she fuh me
Call she fuh me
Call she fuh me

See muh lil brown girl call she fuh me
Tell her I wanna go home[1]

Ring-a-ring o' roses
A pocket full of posies
A-tishoo, aitishoo
We all fall down

Baa baa black sheep
Have you seen Little Bo Peep
Hickety Pickety, my black hen
Lays egg for a gentleman
Three blind mice see how they run
Oh we were having so much fun

And all those old ones

Old MacDonald had a farm
De old lady lived in her shoe
And accidentally swallowed a fly
I think she will die

The farmer in the dell
Saw three blind mice
Chopped off their heads with a carving knife

Johnny get lock up and he en do nothing
Pampalam . . .

My grandmother sprang up like a bullet
Advising us to stop it, stop it.
That was a forbidden song
Words that should never cross our tongues

Refocus
Start a new chorus

Little Sally Waters . . .
Sitting in a saucer
Rise, Sally, rise
Wipe your weeping eyes
Sally turn to the left
Sally turn to the right
Sally turn to the one you like the best

Jack be nimble
Jack be quick
Jack jump over de candle stick

Twenty-four black birds in de air
Papa shoot them day by day
Mama cook them in de pot
Papa eat them like a man
When he done he lick he hand
Mama say what a greedy man
Papa say don't talk too hard
Cause de neighbours in de yard

Miss Mary Mack, Mack, Mack
All dressed in black, black, black

Who stole the cou-cou from de cou-cou jar
#1 stole de cou-cou from de cou-cou jar
Who me?
Not me

All day all night
Ms. Mary Ann

Down by the seaside sifting sand
Even little children love Mary Ann

We sang to the top of our voices
Making music, beautiful noises
Looking up to the sky
Not feeling shy
Twinkle, twinkle little star
You don't look very far

We played as though it was daylight
Dancing under the moon's light

—JLM

Sad News at Assembly

They announced it the morning assembly

Our classmate and friend
Stephen
Killed on the weekend
Struck
By a dump truck

Deafening silence
Echoing

Tears flowing
Weeping

Thinking

Just Friday, we had played ball
Did not have a care at all

Skylarking all over the place
Competing to win every race

He
So small and nimble
Everyone loved his dimples

He exuded joy from within
Always present a cheeky grin

So loveable
Affable
So bright

How could he be gone
Barely twelve years born

I can still see him in his little khaki uniform.

What he would have become
If he had not been
Struck
By a dump truck

Killed on the weekend
Adorable, loveable

Stephen

—JLM

The Visit

The taxi stopped in front of our house
We stared as timid as a mouse would
Out stepped a well-dressed man
Fancy suitcase in his hand

He came up and knocked at the door
The suitcase and leather bag in tow
My grandmother came from the kitchen
Stood staring silently at him

He flung both arms akimbo
Like he was ready to dance flamenco
Gasped and said what's happening here
The entire house was in complete disarray

My grandmother looked really sad
Asked him not to be so mad
Explained that the house was under repair
That's why things were everywhere

He started looking all around
His mouth slowly becoming a frown
My grandmother started to cry
But invited him to come inside

We stood there watching silently
Who could this rude stranger be
We just wanted him to go away
Definitely did not want him to stay
As though he was reading our thoughts
He started acting as he ought

Took a glance at all of us
Said sorry for making such a fuss

We stepped back to allow him in
On his face was now a little grin
Then it became an outright smile
He was making an effort to reconcile

He wanted this visit to be a surprise
Planned to walk up and knock twice
My grandmother would look out
And give a big delighted SHOUT

HEY SON, welcome home

We were filled with glee
And, oh, so pleased

The man now sitting at our table
Was our one and only uncle

—JLM

Pitching Marbles

The ideal place to be
Is really under a shaded tree
Or in the middle of de road
Though some residents may oppose

Take a piece of chalk
Or a nearby plant stalk
Placed between the big and second toe
Go around really steady and slow
Now look see behold a miracle
You drew a perfect circle

Sometimes call the ring
Other times the ling

Turn and go in the opposite direction
Join the waiting boys already in position
Standing behind a chalked white line
All holding an object of a similar design

In some pockets were
hidden treasures
Giving the owner utopian pleasures

Cherry seeds
Steelies
Flakies
Pretties

Big taws

Invoking awe!

Knees, hips and knuckles
They are all ready to pitch marbles

Like every game there are rules
Know them ... dont be the fool

Each boy had placed a marble in the ring

Now a prized and coveted thing

Ready, aim, concentrate

Every marble a target

Plenty schemes are now afoot

Not one will pitch by the book

The goal is to win every marble in that ring

Show the entire village you are the king

With a determining chuckle

The marble is placed on the knuckle

Speed

    Velocity

        Accuracy

           Dexterity

              Some trickery

Ingredients

Requirements

That will catapult that object

To reach the intended subject

Waiting in the ring

For the marble king

—JLM

Sticks 'N Stones

May break my bones

But words will never hurt

A mechanism

And chasm

Trapping the words

Forming phrases

Sentences

Written on the leaves

Of our lives

That we read

N

Repeat

To the next

Generation

—JLM

Beholden

They would notice
Your budding breasts
Before you did

Watch your every step
Take away your innocence
With their stare

The exuberance of
Development
Dissipates

And becomes a
Stifling
Weight

As they wait
And watch
And watch

The eye
Brims
Full

Overflows
To the
Lips

Helpless
To contain
Candied

Words that
Will be aimed
At unsuspecting
Ears

You
Looking
Good
Girl

Startled

Awake

Unnerved

Scared

Scarred

—JLM

The Silent O

Not happy with that doctor!
Told my sister not to bother
Not to worry about that

It is only body fat

Even as it got bigger
And her midsection got fuller

Send her back home every time
Convince her that all was fine

Latently, laid a giant beast
Waiting on an innocent body to feast
Silently squirting droplets of venom
In a cavity of the abdomen
Tests soon confirmed every fear
A deadly creature was indeed lying there

TEARS, TEARS!

Ahead of us

A Herculean task

Options

Choices
Fast

Deliberation
Consultation
Discussions

How best to approach the BEAST
And its entire being seize

TEARS, TEARS

Let us go inside
See what should be applied

It was fully entrenched
Everywhere drenched
Like sticky rice is what they said
Nestled cozy in its own putrid bed

After the surgery
Chemotherapy

REPRIEVE

Glory be
We started to breathe
Laugh, live

Alas . . .

Every method proved in vain
The BEAST fully reigned
It was in total control
Its poison slowly taking hold

The savage beast was out of control

Combative
Aggressive
Resistant
Non-compliant

TEARS, TEARS, TEARS

Methodically

It devoured her body
Leaving a shell only

Barely able to move or stir
Whispered "I am going through there"

Closed her eyes

We watched as she took that last breath
And silently and peacefully left us

Not happy with that doctor
Told my sister not to bother
Not to worry about that

It is only body fat

—JLM

Forever in Our Hearts, Diana

Diana, the years have just flown by
But the pain and the tears did not subside
Diana, it seems like you've gone 'long,
Leaving us here with tears furlong
But as we weep at every thought that triggers memories of you
We hear you chuckle: "Don't worry, I coming 'long too!"

On our Australia–New Zealand trip
We often called your name on the plane, on the bus, train and ship:
"Diana would do this," or, "Diana would do that," we would say
'Cause we feel your presence every minute of the day

When we talk about the sights and sounds
We hear you say: "I enjoyed that too"
But you've got to see this other place where immense beauty and
joy abounds
"You aint gotta worry 'bout schedules, visas, taxes or anything so
'Cause life where I am is hassle-free with joy galore"

Yesterday as we took to the town
Seems like you were on target
Cause just as we reached that store
There was this guitar man outside the door singing Eric Clapton's "No
tears in Heaven"
We stopped and listened as our tears silently flowed
And do you know what was strange about our experience at this store?
When we were exiting that song was again the guitar man's repertoire!

So we moved on with fresh tears aflow
But comforted ourselves with the thought that you were
supernaturally present

With your big trademark smile aglow

You are forever in our hearts, Diana!

—*CHERIL MARSHALL-MORRIS*

Mud

Sun
Sky
Sea

Butt naked
Romping
Free

Children from the motherland
Enjoying their new found island

Sun, sky, sea
And sometimes mud
Gifts from God above

MUD

Pile the dirt up high
We shall make mud pies

Make a hole in the middle
Add water and you have a puddle

Jump to your heart's delight
Not an adult in sight

Next

Grab an old baking pan
A piece of stick in one hand

Stir dirt and water together
No need for salt or sugar

Lovely

Black cake

SKY

Let it sit for a while

SUN

It will be fully baked

SEA!   Surrounded by it

—JLM

My Son's Visit

Blue skies, fresh breezes, and lots of sun

A world of laughter and fun

People smile at you and say hello

Even though you don't live next door

My parents are from this land

How I love its beaches and pearly white sand

In the summer, I hurry down there fast

And try to connect with my parents' past

I always hear them talk about their navel string

And the melodious calypsos they use to sing

I visit all their favourite spots and places

And enjoy the wind in the open spaces

I love the mauby, the cou-cou, and flying fish

Black pudding and souse is a delectable dish

Conkies, pone, stew dumplings, and sweet bread

Cut a green coconut and put it to your head

Mangoes, apples, ackees, sweet and sour plums

I am yet to sip Cockspur or Mount Gay rum

I am talking about a place called Barbados

Thank God He keeps it safe for each of us

Oh little rock, you are part of my inheritance

This makes me feel proud and oh so important

If you left and never even bothered to go back

Just hurry home right now and start to pack

—JLM

De Topsy 'N De Chamberpot

I like being under this bed
You can hear everything being said
Yeah, what about all the sounds we hear
Sometimes they fuhget we so near
Groaning en moaning en funny sounds
En then de mattress going up en down
Could be an earthquake
Or something faked
Doesn't matter
Don't you bother
We got each other
Give me your handle
Life can be wonderful
We got all night
When they turn off de light

—JLM

An Excursion

Was every Barbadian delight
It was like a passage of rite

Out would come the pretty pans
Sent years ago from England

Containing assorted sweeties'n toffees
Wafers and delectable cookies

Now empty, but still brand new
We grandmothers always kept more than a few

Now packed tight with corn beef sandwiches
Pudding and sweet bread all thinly sliced

Can't forget de cassava pone
Not after grating your fingers to de bone

Rice'n peas wrapped in blankets
Packed securely in homemade cane lily baskets

Two less fowls in de backyard
Yuh sneak in late de night before and ketch dem off guard

Now baked brown and succulent sweet
Everything packed except the head and the feet

A glass bottle securing the gravy
Keeping it safe and warm for the journey

De women pretty in brand new dress
Fussy with hair all coiffed and newly pressed

Men well-groomed and looking dapper
Clothing and footwear in style and proper

Children already dressed and sitting quietly
Grinning from ear to ear and fidgeting excitedly

But we knew

To sit there

And not move
Nor skylark
Nor get in de way
Or rumple our clothes
Or ask questions
OR M.O.V.E.

De adults would not A.P.P.R.O.V.E

They would make you stay home
All by yourself all alone

So we knew the drill
Sit here very S.T.I.L.L.

Until it's time to get on de bus
Orderly and without making a fuss

They taking us to
River Bay
Or
Archer's Bay

Or King George the V Memorial Park

Or De Crane

No matter where

We can't wait to get there

We will have lots of fun
At de excursion

—JLM

Kites

Easter is coming, Easter is coming
Kites will be flying, flying, flying

Up, up and away, away
High, high in the air, air
Everywhere!

Giant kites, big kites, small kites
Some almost out of everyone's sight
Might!

All the colours of the rainbow

Flying high
Waving to the earth below, below
Glow!

—JLM

Lover of Kites

Weekend, Easter, summer, Christmas vacations

These were all spent in kite heaven

Small kites
Medium kites
Large kites
Round, square, or oblong
He made kites morning noon or night
Flying them until it was no longer daylight
Kites made of bread paper or book leaves
Kites with bones and kites without
This was his passion no doubt

Some with mad bulls, some bare
As long as he had his kites, he did not have a care

He used good dress bands for kite tails
This resulted in lashes without fail
Admonished by his parents not to go out in the sun
The minute they left home, this warning was spurned
The lover of kites needed to get his fix
He just didn't bother about the licks
Summer vacation fun was going to the sea
But for this young boy it was kites, kites, flying free
He'd come into the house looking all sun-kissed
Fully aware of the consequences of his kiting bliss
He is a grown man with a son of his own
Here is hoping he passes on his kite obsession

—*VERLYNE V FORDE*

An Ounce of Cheese

The cheese was sliced so thin

It could be carried away by the wind

Oh, the shock to realise

You can see all the way to Bathsheba when you hold it to your eyes

He'd stand about two feet away from the scale

And toss it in the middle of the scale pan without flail

The poise would clang loudly with a bang

While other patrons in the shop stand

Before the poise could register the weight

The cheese was removed and wrapped, leaving one wondering if it should be used for bait

—VERLYNE V FORDE

The Shopkeeper

Once or twice a month he visited the city and replenished his stock

He departed around 7 o'clock, nodding a greeting to those waiting at the bus stop

By 11:30 a.m. he was back behind the counter

Packing away his purchases and serving his patrons with fervour

If you are planning to make chicken soup on those stock-up days

Don't count on the shopkeeper to satisfy your crave

He looks at you as if in a daze

Two pounds of chicken back you say?

Just got back from the city and its not frozen yet

Tomorrow would be your best bet

—*VERLYNE V FORDE*

The Drunken Choir

They gathered together late Friday and Saturday evenings

This was their way of socialising

Each guy would buy a round

They'd cheer each other as they toss it down

Half way through the get together an argument may ensue

Whether it be politics and the latest item on the news

Out of the blues the music scale could be heard

As they trained their voices . . .

Do re mi fa sol la ti do

These tipsy men were about to start a show

In unison, they sang hymn after hymn

This was an indication they were rounding off the entertaining

Each person held his own as they sang as a group: bass, alto, and tenor

There was no indication of a slur

They share the last bottle and clinked their glasses

Wishing each other good night and God's blessings

They departed, each going his separate way

Some stepping high and some staggering

God's speed until next Friday evening

As I learn to play the trumpet in my later years

The music scale heard from the drunken choir so long ago,

Still ring in my ears

Do   re   mi   fa   sol   la   ti   do

—*VERLYNE V FORDE*

Delicacies

Sky, sea, sand, and sun
An assortment of Bajan rum
Grab yourself some fish cakes
A glass of Mauby and some bakes
Oh, and then there's macaroni pie
Or cou-cou with fish—steamed or fried
On Saturday at almost every house
You will find pudding'n souse
Grab a Ju-C, a plus, or a Banks beer
Relaxing on a beach right here

Barbados

Beautiful'n waiting for you

—JLM

Primary School

Be standing in that perfect line
When de school bell ring at nine
Ready to say De Lord's Prayer 'n sing
Or bare lashes in yuh little behind

Mek sure yuh finger nails short and clean
Not a speck of dirt or mud must be seen
Ready to say De Lord's Prayer 'n sing
Or some hot lashes in yuh little behind.

Don't forget yuh slate at home

Your hair must be combed

Ready to say De Lord's Prayer 'n sing
Or bare lashes in yuh little behind

No dog ears in your exercise book
It is important how it looks

Ready to say De Lord's Prayer 'n sing

Or some hot lashes in yuh little behind

Always remember to say Please, Teacher

Never be rude to your leader

Ready to say De Lord's Prayer 'n sing

Or bare lashes in yuh little behind

—JLM

Ballahoo, Heartman, Duppy

When I was growing up in the Caribbean

Lots of things frightened me man

There were duppies, de heartman, and de ballahoo

Real scary things I wish I could tell you

Legends that are part of Barbados' history

Stories told to me at my grandparents' knee

Children we were, wishing to hear more

Fascinated and thrilled by these old folklore

De heartman lived in the growing canes

Not caring if there was sun or rain

Had the title of the devil's right-hand man

Cruised around in a black car or a fancy fan

The one objective he had in mind

A wandering own way child to find

He would rip out your heart or your soul

And present them to the devil in a bowl

Ballahoo was a type of mythical creature

Big as a calf but had a dog-like feature

Made its appearance with clanging chains

Had power to inflict quite a dosage of pain

Caused rocks to fall on your rooftop

Could make anybody's underwear drop

When the ballahoo was set on you

It was for debt or payments long overdue

Duppies only came out late at night

Their bones and sinews could not take sunlight

They would assume any shape or form

No one was to expect the norm

They could creep into the house

Quiet and stealthily as a mouse

Any dog howling or growling late at night

God, help us a duppy somewhere in sight.

I can still recall those bright moonlight nights

My heart pounding, my body trembling with fright

But hoping those stories would never end

Glad I was among family and friends

Ever so often, glancing all around

Jumping out of my skin at the slightest sound

Planning when it was time to go to bed

I was placing the Bible right at my head.

—JLM

The Centipede

Stealthily like a mouse

It crept into our house

Like a horror picture

That multi-leg creature

We spotted it on the floor

Screamed and bolted for the door

But my grandmother knew no fear

Smirked as it sped away

She grabbed the Flit can

Headed in the direction it ran

Kerosene oil filled the air

The house was bombarded with spray

The creature staggered from a space

Alas, there was no hiding place

Moving now like a snail

Leaving behind an oily trail

She observed it inch along

No longer moving strong

Watched it until

Finally

It laid still

One final blow to its head

Ensured the creature was really dead

—JLM

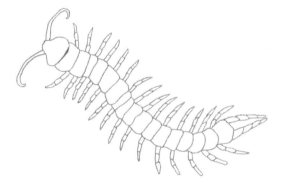

T'was De Nite before Christmas

It was always de night before Christmas

In every house lots of ado and even more fuss

Cobweb brooms packed away

Every windowpane shinning bright as day

Brand new linoleum purchased the day before

Lay sparkling on the scrubbed wooden floor

Cabinets, couches, chairs gleaming with varnish

Giving the impression the house was newly furnished

All around was a vision of an overseas Christmas card

Local government had inadvertently provided the marl

The pig in the backyard grunted in content

Not knowing his last hours were being spent

A resounding bass, tenor, soprano, falsetto

In perfect harmony a Christmas carol would echo

The men slightly tipsy returning from the local shop

Without doubt it had to be nine o'clock

A million things completed, still so much to do

Christmas better not come before we were through

Baking pans to be found, washed, and greased

Bowls of ungrated coconuts to be peeled

Containers of green peas still to be shelled

I did not like jug jug, but I dared not tell

Brand-new curtains pressed, yet to be hung

With these we dared not messed around

Tradition dictated they be hung one hour prior to dawn

Neighbours could not see them before Christmas morn

Patiently, silently, we waited in our little world

Waiting for the Christmas activities to unfurl

Lots of pudding and sweet bread to be baked

And my favourite—a spiced up rummy black cake

Delicious smells would soon permeate the air

Giving a savoury welcome to an imminent Xmas day

A slice of ham, a taste of the cake and the pudding

A foretaste of the goodies that would be soon coming

Finally, a good night would be said

And we'd go contently to our beds

One more peek at my new shoes and pretty dress

Tomorrow, I would be looking so nice and fresh

In a few hours, we would rise with the sun

To a day filled with much laughter and fun

Santa would not be sliding down our chimney

That was not part of our reality, or our society

No Christmas trees, no presents, or toys

Maybe a harmonica or a new cap—if you were a boy

To our minds, our hearts, this did not matter at all

Our Christmas did not depend on

Santa Claus making a call

—JLM

A Nut Seller's Creed

Downsizing, reducing, eliminating

Everybody being forced into entrepreneuring

Ere, these words were popular

I was my own sole proprietor

Balancing my business on my head

Life wasn't easy it must be said.

Working through hot sun and pouring rain

Many times, I tell you, I was in dire pain

Nuts, toffees, popcorn, mints

I built up my assets cent by cent

Adding, subtracting, making change in my head

I hardly ever had to use a black lead

No CEO to give me an ounce of advice

I, alone, figuring out selling and cost price

Supply and demand, the economists say

Each day I had to decide what to put on my tray

Big business discarding longtime employees

Could swear we reverting to feudal society

Those few left behind are assigned multiple tasks

Expecting to perform like a hired-out jackass

Excessive, extravagant profits are all that matters

Who cares if people's damn lives are in tatters

Downsizing, reducing, eliminating

Everybody being forced into entrepreneuring

You can call me speculator, hawker, nut seller

I say to you, I am the original 'sole proprietor'

—JLM

Duppies

Bones and sinews

Cannot take sunlight

So

They come out at night

Staying out of sight

Following you to your door

Hiding in the ceiling or the floor

Each person required a way

To keep those duppies at bay

You won't be considered a coward

Spin around and walk in backward

Sleep with your jammies on the wrong side

Pray that God with you abide

Dogs howling incessantly at night

Was a sign that duppies were in sight

Grandparents told of hearing running feet

But seeing no one or nothing on the street

Told us it had to be the duppy in a hurry

Trying to get back to the cemetery

Imagine our plight

We lived in fright

The stories we would hear

Filled us with fear

Yet we could not get enough

Of this frightening, scary stuff

—JLM

My Love, My Everything

To be in love is a wonderful thing

Not puppy love or a casual thing

But loving with all our hearts

And only death can tear us apart

Joined as one

In matrimonial bond

Something new, borrowed, something blue

We hereby declare my undying love for you

In vigour and in health

For riches and for wealth

You are the sunshine of my life

Committed as husband and wife

You are de peas in my rice

De cheese in my mac pie

De fish in my fish cakes

De flour in my bakes

De corn meal in my cou-cou

De dasheene in my callaloo

De beef in my rotis

De pumpkin in my conkies

De meat in my pepper pot

Spicy and blazing hot

Turmeric in my pepper sauce

Without you I am lost

De dumplings in my soup

Sweet potato and breadfruit

Cassava, eddoes, okras, and yams

De jelly in my coconut

Just picked and newly cut

Apples, mangoes, plums, guavas

Fat porks, cashews, carambola

Dunks, tamarinds, ackees

Grapefruit, shaddock, and cherries

Soursop, bananas, gooseberries

De fruits and product of every tree

Sugar pie, sweet plum, honey bunch

You are my dinner, breakfast, my lunch

Mauby, lemonade, or ginger beer

Honey, we are an awesome pair

In a nutshell, to be concise and precise

You are the vanilla essence of my life

From this day onward

We only moving forward

—*JLM*

Local Stand Pipe

A cultural landmark all over the island
Bequeathed by the government

Used by everyone
But owned by none

Water provided free for all
From a cement-looking stall

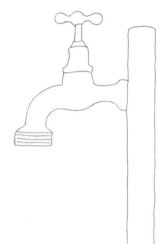

With galvanized bucket in hand
Skillet or a giant wash pan

Women and children made their way
Lugging and carrying water during the day

Squabbles and fights would sometimes ensue
Disagreement and resentment took root and grew

Secrets and confidences breached and exposed
Became narratives to be shared and retold

Rumours and gossip were hatched or born
With time took on a life of their own

Some women developed lasting friendships
Created by conversations during these trips

Many relationships got started at these sites
And romance blossomed to everyone's delight

Late in the evening, men took their baths
Hoping no one would come pass

Shampoo resting on the floor on the stall
Blue or Lux soap somewhere on the wall

Many unsuspecting and innocent eyes
Blinking and trying to contain surprise

Certain body parts would be seen by chance
Since one could not resist a quick and furtive glance

Every mother warning her young daughter
Remember the words of wisdom taught to her

See no evil, speak no evil, hear no evil, do no evil
Avoid all temptation and cause no upheaval
All had a vested interest in this establishment
Knew its importance to all the inhabitants

Build solid and to last
A fundamental aspect of our past.

—JLM

Coconut Trees

Ever since I fell from that coconut tree
I developed an affinity

Behold these majestic trees
Swaying gently in the early morning breeze

Lush and oh, so verdant green
Nothing nobler has been seen

God waving to us from high above
Declaration of His eternal love

The trunks stretch tall and gaunt
Sometimes a few slightly bent
Palms and fronds protectively encircle
The offspring of their navels

God waving to us from high above
Declaration of His eternal love

Observe as nature its mystery begins
Coconut water and jelly and their origins

The succulent white matter within
And the liquid combine for a perfect blend

God waving to us from high above
Declaration of His eternal love

Food and drink provided to us
Encased in green or brown husk

God waving to us from high above
Declaration of His eternal love

—JLM

Bakes

I so love bakes

Simple to make

Easier and faster than cake

Sift your flour

Sprinkle a lil spice

Add sugar and salt

Blend with enough water

To ensure the mixture

Is malleable to drop in

The frying pan

Already sitting on the stove

With the cooking oil

Scoop the mixture in a spoon

Drop in the pan

And fry until golden brown

One of those flexible foods

That is oh, so good

—JLM

Conkies

A Bajan delicacy
Wrapped in a banana leaf
And steamed slowly

Blend

Of
2 cups of cornmeal
1 cup of grated pumpkin
1 cup of grated coconut
1 cup of milk
½ cup of grated potato
1 cup of sugar
1 tbs of cinnamon
1 tbs of nutmeg
6 oz of butter or margarine
Salt

Add

Some cranberries
And raisins

If you want

Mix the grated items together
Add the other items after
Stir and blend it really well
When it's ready, you can tell

The leaves need to be supple
So they don't give trouble
The batter should fit snugly inside
And not be spilling on the outside

So

Hold the leaves slightly over the fire
Until they start to lose the green colour
Should be flexible to your touch
Yet not easy to break or crush

Place the batter on the leaf
Fold like it was a sleeve
Repeat till all the batter is done

Any left over can be frozen

A reminder they must be steamed
And not cooked to the extreme
Do not place directly in the water
They won't cook as they oughta

Now you are almost finished
Your delicacy soon to relish

A Bajan delicacy
Steamed in a banana leaf

Bon appetit

—JLM

Raised by the Village

The village

It was global

Everybody

Knew

You

Your

Grandfather

Grandmother

Mother

Father

Genealogy

And your baobab tree

Kept

You

On the straight and narrow

Like Cupid's arrow

They

Could and would

Ring your ears

Slap you hard

Thump you down

Then send you home

'Cause they saw you on the street

Acting like a deadbeat

Would and could

Administer a father's correction

A mother's direction

'Cause

You

Talking back and strupsing your mout

And carrying on like a lout

Looking me in the face

Walking by like you in a race

Not even a common greeting

Like good morning

Afternoon

Or good evening

Not even yuh dog, yuh cat

How yuh behaving like that?

Show some broughtupsy

Decency

Pleasantry

How come you all up here

You don't live up this way

Don't hasten yuh pace

I recognise de face

You is Ms. Thing grandchild

Yuh still got yuh mother smile

I know yuh when you was this high

Hiding behind yuh grandmother, acting shy

Look how tall you get

En lose yuh mother features yet

Would give the shirts off their backs

Even if and when they lacked

Would give their last penny

Even if they did not have money

They were not really mean

Simply the Village Team

Who cared

Allayed our fears

Wiped our tears

Wished only good for us

And for us to be safe

In the village

—JLM

The Rediffusion

Barbados, the first British colony
To have the Rediffusion Service in the 1930s

That little brown box

Hung in the corner of our dining room

Pivotal

Essential

Crucial

Available and accessible to all

A tapestry of sound and art

News

Weather

Sports

Oh the knowledge to us it did impart

It brought the world to our ears

World affairs

Politics

Entertainment

Educated us throughout the years

DJs with voices like silk

Every genre of music that exist

Was part of their play list

Showcased diversity and other cultures

Covered everything that mattered

World news from the BBC

Music to remember
In the middle of the weekday
Classical, quiet, sombre
Bach, Beethoven, Brahms, Chopin
Mozart, Tchaikovsky
Names that intrigued and
Filled with wonder

Title fights
Muhammad Ali, our favourite
My grandfather
Fist clinched tight

Hoping someone would knock
That Cassius out
Shut up his boastful mout

How dare he beat
Sonny Liston
His hands moving like pistons

Friday nights we
Sang

Danced
To the songs
Of the *Hit Parade*

Saturday
Races
From
De Garrison Savannah
Children's Party

Cricket
From
Kensington Oval
Australia
England
New Zealand
Other Caribbean islands
Pakistan
South Africa

Sunday
A
Time of
Hymns
And
Worship

Quiet
Reflective

Reminding
Us to
Relax

Rest
Recuperate

Go to
Church

The little brown box

Pivotal

Essential

Crucial

Hugs 'N Kisses

Did not want my dear old aunt

Kissing me

Would avoid her embrace

Break free

So what if she looked heart broken

And was only trying

To

Show

Affection

I am dancing to the drums of my youth

Things to do

Places to go

Peoples to see.

Aint got time fuh she

Now here I be

Youth has no loyalty

And has waltz on with another

Found some new partners

My nieces and nephews

Dancing to its beat

Things to do

Places to go

Peoples to see

Aint got no time

For

Kisses

From

M

E

—*JLM*

Grand Dames

Agatha Zipporah

Louise Ambrozine

Grand dames

Caring

Loving

Nurturing

With all their hearts

Grandmothers

Women like no other

Wiping tears with hands that are kind

Smiling eyes that say you are mine

Cuddling you with tenderness

Only concern with your happiness

Flesh of their flesh

Bone of their bone

From the moment we are born

And even when we are grown

They keep us in their embrace

One that defies time and space

Grandmothers

Dependable

Responsible

Reliable

Love

Unfailing

Abiding

Eternal

God

Encapsulated

—JLM

A Grandmother's Love

Like the sun's ray
Radiating on a sunny day

Iridescent

Dazzling

Stars in the sky
Wide and vast

Luminous
Spherical

Solid

Compact

Eternal

—JLM

The Sweetest Evenings

Books borrowed from the Mobile Library
On loan for two weeks, and it was all free
Such a wide variety from which to choose
And the options to renew

Sitting around the giant table
Listening to Aesop's Fables
Lots of once-upon-a-time stories
And fascinating Greek mythology

Zeus, Apollo, Atlas, Hercules
Athena, Aphrodite, Icarus, Hermes
God's goddesses, deities
Filled with power and mastery
Stories of such intrigue
You could not help but read
Pandora defiant and sly as a fox
Opening and peeking in that forbidden box
Evil and sickness and ills escaped
Only hope was left as the human drape

Adventures from the *Arabian Nights*
Depicting suffering and human plight
Alibaba concealed by the forest leaves
Watched in total surprise and utter disbelief
As forty thieves hid stolen treasures in a cave
Believing it was secure and safe
Learned the power of the words Open Sesame
Outsmarted them and became very wealthy

The huge Maccabee Bible
With books and unfamiliar titles
Colourful and beguiling pictures
Of the Old Testament characters

Adam and Eve in the garden of Eden
Sinned and could not be pardoned
Eternal banishment was their fate
An angel standing guard at the gate

Cain killed his brother Abel
And was destined for hell

Noah building a giant ark
From wood and gopher bark

Jonah was swallowed by a whale
And lived to tell the tale
Joseph and his multicoloured coat
His brothers almost cut his throat
Moses, the baby hidden in a basket
His sister tasked to look after it
David slayed Goliath with his sling
And went on to become a king
Daniel was thrown in a lion's den
And God their jaws suspend

All about men of might and valour
I guess women did not matter

Tales of such wild adventures
Filled our hearts with awe and wonder

It was in the quiet of the twilight
To every one of our hearts delight

My grandmother's voice

Comforting

    Soft

        Sweet

           and

              Oh

                So

                  Mellow

In the lamp's warm luminous glow

—JLM

The Christmas Worm

It would appear from nowhere
Inching along the wooden floor
Going without concern or fear
Oblivious to our thankful stares

What was its purpose in life?
Where did it really reside?
How did it survive?
Why so small in size?

It seemed so inconsequential
But its sighting was essential
Here is the convincing reason
It was the advent to the Christmas season

—JLM

Good Times

There were good times
Telling jokes times
Dancing to the *Hit Parade* times
Listening to cricket times
Playing hopscotch times
Bringing water together times
Going to school together times
Going to church together times

They were the best of times
Truly the best of times

Were we poor
Maybe so

But we were never notified

It was not a bother
We had each other

A tight bond of familyship
A generation of kindred spirit

Seven siblings
Six first cousins
More than a baker's dozen

We had our own cricket team
Every neighbourhood's dream

We pitched marbles
Collected sweet drink bottles

Played tennis
On the road's hard surface
Exciting and tremendous
Like Serena and Venus

Climbed trees
Picked peas

Ran with the cows
Though it was not allowed

Ate each other's food
Laughing as we chewed

We lived by the family's established rule
Which we accepted as really cool

One for all
And
All for one

Until life is DONE

—JLM

I So LOVE Bakes

Say!

I so love bakes
Bajan I am

I can eat them every day
Especially on Saturdays

Here
There
Anywhere
Everywhere

Outside
Inside

Try them
You will like them

Sitting on concrete
Standing on a beach

In the sun
With a sip of rum

By the lake
With a piece of cake

On a plane
In a train

With a chicken leg
Or scrambled egg

Try them
You will like them

Slice of ham
Or guava jam

Bacon strips
Sweet potato chips

A piece of cheese
Thanks and please

With peas 'n rice
Or macaroni pie

A plate of beef stew
Smiling while I chew

Anytime
Is just fine

Try them
You will like them

Bakes

Try them
You will like
Them

Anytime
Every time

Here
There

Anywhere
Everywhere

Outside
Inside

Try Them
You will like
Them

I so
Love
Bakes

Bajan
I
Am

—JLM

Fish, Fish, Flying Fish

Fish, fish, fish
Fresh from de sea
Plentiful like peas

See the big car driving by
Everyone hearing his cry
Fish, fish, flying fish

Women running with a pail
Can't miss out on this sale
Fish, fish, flying, fish

One hundred for a dollar
Life could not be better
Fish, fish, flying fish

Clean them

Steam some
Fry Some

Wings
Melts
Seasoning packed around de straight bone

Fish, fish, flying fish

Sit

Eat
To your heart's delight

Fish
Fish
Flying fish

—*JLM*

June '74

The foundation
Of our
Lives was
Shaken to the core

Death, the
Unwelcomed guest
Barged through our door

What an
Ugly face

Those crusty
Manicured hands

Took our grand

Mother

Leaving
In her absence

A presence

Of stabbing pain

Tears flowing
Like rain

A hole
Tearing
At our souls

Our grand
Mother

Lying still

Unmoving

Hands
That had

Bathed
Tended
Cared
We could
Not comprehend

Lips
That had

Snuggled
Smiled

Now
Slacked

What about tomorrow?
We were filled with sorrow

Staring with disbelief

Knowing our grief
Would never be
Brief

—JLM

Summer of '75

It was the summer of '75
My aunt and her children arrived

From England

For us, a long-anticipated trip
Opportunity to cement kinship

We had never seen each other or met
And were not sure what to expect

It was love at first sight
We were filled with delight

Our three cousins were so much fun
We romped and played in the sun
Wendy with her brand-new tape deck
Seem to have it attached to her neck

Introduced us to a different world
We danced, whirled, twirled

Sang along
To Bob Marley
Popular song

No, woman, no cry
Sing it we did try

She had wigs of many colours
Invoking awe and wonder

Mini skirts and platform shoes
Made us wish we had the same too

Our aunt had made it all happen
More magical than we could ever imagine

Bringing our cousins to our lives
In the summer of '75

—JLM

De Coconut

The most significant thing I did today
Was to cut a coconut
To tell de truth

It was there . . . and I tell myself
I don't want it to spoil

It took me a while to scrub de collins
And sanitize it
Since de collins was out dey in de yard for a while
I scrub it down and douse it wid boiling water
Just in case de rat or mouse had run over it
I wasn't taking any chances
In de back of mind
I see a collins as a death threat
Like it was fuh my Fadda

He and his friend cut a coconut
And he end up with leptospirosis

Now it is true we do have a few coconut trees

But, this one coconut was lying around for two or three days
In just a matter of time it would be bilgy

If I don't use it
It would go bad

When it start to go down
It was good

In Bajan parlance
I met it there
It touch the spot

—*COLVIN JABEZ MARSHALL* (RIP)

Lord, Have Mercy

On Sundays, my Grandmother would pray
Her heart filled with fear

Lord, don't let de PIPE lock off
Before I finish wash de rice

Christmas mornings, my Grandfather would pray
His heart filled with fear

Lord, don't let de PIPE lock off
Before de butcher finish kill this pig and we clean it up

During de week, my aunt would pray
Lord don't let de PIPE lock off before I rinse out de clothes

Today, more than fifty years later. this is my pray
Lord, don't let de PIPE lock off on Christmas Day

—JLM

The Clamacherry Tree

Its branches spreading wide

Like the ocean's vast tide

The cherries hanging in clusters

With a shiny ripe brown lustre

Colonies of ants on every limb

Concealing themselves on the rim

Like paid sentries always on guard

Trying to keep us from the backyard

A well-organized inf-ant-ry

With a foolproof strategy

The red ones' bite would sting like fire

The black ones' bite always seem tamer

One group would bite and roll

The other would bite and fold

Each finding a hiding place

Be it your hand or your face

But we the children of the sun

Would not be outdone

We did not care about the stings

Getting the cherries was our thing

They provided that adhesive glue

And that is what we did pursue

To fix our torn books and make kites

At times we'd give the cherries little bites

Sometimes climb the branches

Plucked those cherries by the batches

Then behold your hands and faces

Swatting the ants from their hiding places

Such fond memories of that beautiful

Clamacherry tree

Its massive branches spreading wide

Like the ocean's vast tide

—JLM

Rihanna's Dress

People are talking about Ri-Ri's braless orange/gold dress
Saying how it was inappropriate cause all her 'girls' were unharness
What they really do not understand
Is that Ri-Ri knows just how to play her hand

Understand that she's not about satisfying people's etiquette
or diplomacy
'Cause truth be told, not much of that brings in a penny
. . . at least not in her industry
So while we complain, dress-down, fret, and remain brek
Ri-Ri is still drawing in her money
'Cause she understands the difference between town and country.

We seem to be here thinking 'small island' thoughts
While Ri-Ri's brain is on the international lofts
If she auctions that dress, it will sure earn her lots of money
All because it was on her beautiful body.

So, people, try to understand what she means
about 'pon de replay' and 'shine bright like a diamond'
Those are her mantras—overt or covert, vex or please
(**And as Aunty Mia would say "At the end of the day" or "Don't get
tie up"**)
Ri-Ri's modus operandi is all about HER vision and mission and not
what we say or feel

—CHERIL MARSHALL-MORRIS

St. Joseph Uh Come From

St. Joseph uh come from
Romped and played in the sun
Had a childhood of fun

A parish with noteworthy names
A few having worldwide fame

De Soup Bowl for international surfing
Bathesha for bathing or swimming

Tourists gathering at this location
To view and admire the Atlantic Ocean

The curling face of the wave is the Bowl
The whitewater after breaking waves—is de Soup

Then there are all those hills
Walking them called for skills

Airy Hill
Bissex Hill
Bowling Alley Hill
Braggs Hill
Cleavers Hill
Fruitful Hill
Gaggs Hill
Horse Hill
Mellowes Hill
Melvin Hill
Parris Hill
Spa Hill

Spa Hill is the place I was born
Where my formative years were formed

Trees greenery foliage of every kind
Almost every type of fruit you will find

An established church on every corner
And a local (rum) shop for grocery orders

Standing at a towering an impressive 1,083 feet
We boast that Mount Chimborazo is the highest peak

All part of the island wide ongoing rivalry
Between our parish and St. Thomas's Mount Hillaby

St. Joseph—part of the Scotland District
Picturesque, quaint, and totally perfect

To and for me
One hundred per cent Josephine

—JLM

Epilogue

MUD

From the dust of the ground

Was Adam, the first man formed

Our ancestors fed the world

From its black rich fertile soil

It becomes our final resting place

Regardless of our faith or race

We lie there looking up to the

SKY

An extensive canopy of the bluest sky

Etched and decorated by the whitest

Puffiest, clouds the eye could behold

God's blessings painted on a scroll

We behold the

SUN

Hot, sizzling hot

Kissing us most days—bright and radiant

Silent, vibrant, constant, translucent

Granting us warmth, joy, love, freedom

Liberating, welcoming, and awesome

The necessary sunlight for the growth of ground provisions

SEA

Beholding the waters

The Caribbean Sea

And the Atlantic Ocean

Merging

Kissing

Romancing

Blessing us with offspring

Suitably named

Bathsheba

Cattlewash

De Soup Bowl

And so many more beaches

All iridescent in splendour

From January to December

Surrounded by it!

ACKNOWLEDGMENTS

Thanks to God for his many blessings.

And, yes, de whole village contributed to this book of poetry. Bear with me while I say my thanks:

My parents who left for England when we were "little". They wrote to us often. We were required and expected to respond to their letters in a timely fashion. They checked our responses for proper spelling and grammar. Writing (for me) started early uh clock.
Colvin McDonald
Catherine McLean

As I got older and continued my letter writing my mom would say, "the world needs to read your writing".

Hello world! Here I be!

We lived primarily with our maternal grandparents. They could read, write, and reason, but they granted me the opportunity and privilege to read the letters they received from overseas—aunt and uncle who were living in England, my aunt who was living in Canada and, of course, the letters received from our parents

Sometimes, I would be asked to respond to those letters. I would have to read the responses back to them. There were times, when they responded to the letters themselves but would check with us, if they were not sure how to spell a "big word", like pneumonia, or phensic, or pharmacy. Those ambiguous-sounding words.

Agatha Zipporah
Clement Da Costa

There were also those times when my grandfather would wake up on Sunday mornings, before the crack of dawn, to sit quietly at the table and write those responses himself. I can still see him, sitting at the table, writing and writing, and squinting at the air mail envelope as he reread what he had just written. If by chance, we woke up while he was still at this task, we learned how not to breathe too loud or make the slightest sound. He was concentrating on the job.

My grandmother read to us at nights. She made the Old Testament horror stories contained therein interesting and intriguing. My love for the printed word and reading were incubated. No turning back.

My paternal grandparents played their role as well. My grandmother would regale us with duppy stories and riddles that we thought were nonsensical until she gave us the answers, which were always sound and thought-provoking.

Louise Ambrozine
Coleridge

My Aunt Jan ensured we did our schoolwork, washed and "pressed" our school uniforms, cooked and fed us and along with our grandparents, provided us with a safe and comfortable environment for living and learning. In my heart forever and a day—Janet Euretha.

Aunts
Uncle

The Book Mobile (a portable library) came to our area, every two weeks. It would park in a designated area, not far from home. With our grandparents' permission, my older brother would take us there every two weeks.

We selected several books and started reading right away. Two weeks to wait for renewal or to borrow different books always felt like a lifetime.

Every book read was discussed. My older brother always initiated the discussions, plot, subplot, the characters, what made it a good book/story. He made the characters come alive during those discussions.

He was/is an avid reader. He was/is the most influential person in our lives. The perfect big brother.

Over the years, my other siblings have encouraged me in my writing endeavours. They were on my back to get this book going. They all contributed tremendously. Some of the poems herein were written by some of them. My life would be of no consequence without my siblings and the cousins who were such a big part of my childhood.

My sisters
My brother
Cousins

My son got me started by challenging me to write a poem everyday. He drew the illustrations in the book.

My daughter funded the project. The mover and shaker.

My spouse whose wholehearted contributions and involvement in and to the household provides me with the luxury and time to do my writing.

All my in-laws who are family.

My nieces, nephews, and cousins, provided feedback and opinions on the choice of the front cover.

Photo on the front cover taken in the beautiful Island of Barbados, Brandon's Beach.

I also must make mention of the little church, two house spots away from the house in which I was born: Spa Hill New Testament Church. I wrote my first ever skit for that little church on the hill. I received lots of encouragement and support from the elders and my peers alike.

Would this book of poems be possible without the love, influence, help, support of my family, my friends and this village?

I think not.

Thank you, thank you.

You are truly appreciated and loved.

CITATION

1   Farian, Frank. "Brown Girl in the Ring." Rivers of Babylon. Hansa, Sire, Atlantic, 1978. LP

Printed in the USA
CPSIA information can be obtained
at www.ICGtesting.com
JSHW020225261123
R13112700001B/R131127PG52344JSX00001B/1